THE INCAS

SHIRLEE P. NEWMAN
THE INCAS

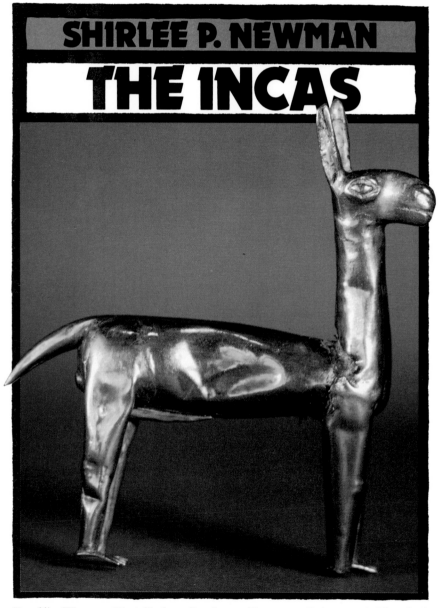

Franklin Watts   New York   London   Toronto   Sydney   A First Book

Map by Joe LeMonnier
Cover photograph copyright © The American Museum of Natural History (#K4771)
Photographs copyright ©: The University Museum, University of Pennsylvania (T4-243c2):
p. 3; The Thomas Gilcrease Institute of American History and Art, Tulsa, Oklahoma: p. 12;
Robert Frerck/Odyssey/Chicago: pp. 14, 15, 30 bottom, 36 bottom, 40; North Wind Picture
Archives: pp. 17, 19, 27, 29, 34 inset, 36 top, 37, 44; Ron Greenberg: pp. 22, 34; The Bettmann
Archive: p. 23; American Museum of Natural History: p. 30 top (#2555-3); The Textile Museum:
p. 32; The Smithsonian Institution: p. 33; Earl Dibble: pp. 46, 53; The Time Museum, Rockford,
Illinois: p. 38; Jack Grove/PhotoEdit: p. 50.

Library of Congress Cataloging-in-Publication Data

Newman, Shirlee Petkin.
The Incas / Shirlee P. Newman.
p.   cm.—(A First book)
Includes bibliographical references (p.   ) and index.
Summary: Describes the civilization of the Inca empire that
flourished from the thirteenth to the sixteenth century and the
present-day lives of the Andean people descended from that empire.
ISBN 0-531-20004-3
1. Incas—Juvenile literature.   2. Quechua Indians—Juvenile
literature.   3. Aymara Indians—Juvenile literature.   [1. Incas.
2. Indians of South America.]   I. Title.   II. Series.
F3429.N485   1992
980'.01—dc20   91-313-78   CIP   AC

4

CONTENTS

For David

THE INCAS

EMPIRE OF THE SUN

Cuzco, a small city in the Andes Mountains of Peru, a country in South America, was once the capital of the Inca civilization, the richest, most powerful empire in all the Americas. At its peak, the Inca empire included Peru, Ecuador, Bolivia, and parts of Argentina, Colombia, and Chile. The empire lasted from about A.D. 1200, when the Incas first entered the valley of Cuzco, to 1532. By that time, millions of natives had died of diseases brought to their shores by white people. The empire had been divided by civil war, and was conquered by the *conquistadores*.

Inca means lord or king. Only members of the royal family could be called Incas in the days of the empire. Today any person belonging to a group once ruled by the Great Inca, or king, is sometimes called an Inca. The word "Indian" is considered an insult in Peru. Natives prefer to be called *runas* or *indigenestas*. Those people

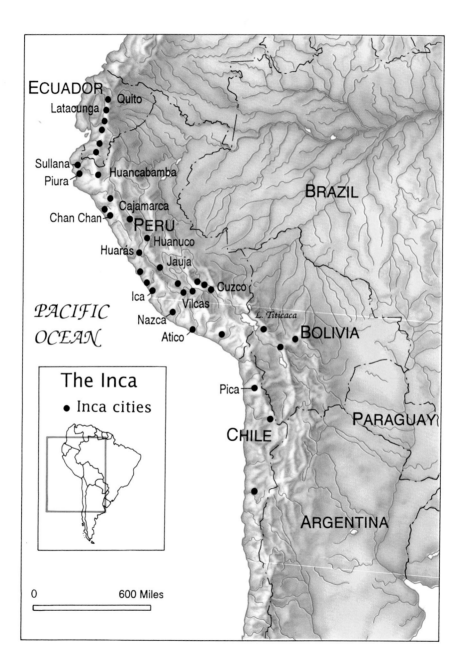

ECUADOR

Quito

Latacunga

Sullana

Piura

Huancabamba

Chan Chan

Cajamarca

PERU

Huanuco

Huarás

Jauja

Ica

Cuzco

Vilcas

Nazca

L. Titicaca

Atico

BOLIVIA

*PACIFIC
OCEAN*

BRAZIL

Pica

CHILE

PARAGUAY

ARGENTINA

The Inca

● Inca cities

0   600 Miles

who farm are often called *campesinos*. Some people are called *Aymaras* or *Quechuas* after the name of the languages they speak.

The Incas are small people with dark hair and almond-shaped eyes. Scientists think they first came to America from the Orient thousands of years ago when there was land between Asia and Alaska.

No one knows for sure how the Inca empire began or whether Manco Capac, the first Great Inca, was real or legendary. One story handed down through the ages says he was born on an island in Lake Titicaca, on the border of Peru and Bolivia. According to another story, Manco Capac stepped out of a cave in the fertile Cuzco valley one morning in the year 1200, wearing a flowing yellow robe and carrying a shiny golden staff.

"I am Manco Capac, son of the Sun God," he is said to have shouted. "My father has sent me to be your leader." According to the story, he flung his staff across the fertile valley and the people there accepted him as their leader.

Whether the story is true or not, Cuzco remained a small farming settlement until 1438. Then a neighboring tribe, called the Chancas, threatened to invade the valley. Pachacuti, the ninth Inca, mobilized an army to keep the Chancas away. He started work on a fortress a short distance from Cuzco to protect the city against invasion.

MANCO CAPAC, THE FIRST GREAT INCA,
MAY HAVE BEEN A REAL PERSON . . .
OR HE MAY HAVE BEEN A LEGEND.

Cuzco became a beautiful capital under Pachacuti. The Incas drained some swampy land and paved a plaza, or square, in the center of the city. They built Pachacuti's palace on the north side and the Temple to the Sun nearby. Archaeologists think Cuzco was planned in the shape of a puma, one of the animals the Incas considered *huaca* (sacred). Beyond the city lies a hill that could represent the puma's head. Here Pachacuti built the fortress. It was called Sacsahuamán and has been called the greatest fortress ever built by native Americans.

The fortress was like a city in itself. It was protected by tall towers and surrounded by enormous walls, some of which still stand. A number of stones in the wall weigh as much as two hundred tons. They were dragged to the site on rollers and fitted together so perfectly that a penknife can't be slipped between them. The stones had to be hoisted into place with nothing but ropes and sheer muscle power. A constant supply of fresh water was carried through underground channels up to the Great Inca's residence, one of many buildings in the fort. Warriors' barracks were connected by underground passageways. There was a maze of streets above ground.

Archaeologists think it took twenty thousand men some sixty years to build Sacsahuamán. By the time it was finished, Pachacuti had died and his son and grand-

THE FORTRESS SACSAHUAMAN,
WHICH MEANS "HIGH-GROUND-
TO-ATTACK-WHICH-PROVIDES-
CORPSES-FOR-VULTURES"

THIS IS THE BEST PRESERVED
INCA WALL, SIMILAR TO THE
WALLS THAT SURROUNDED
THE GREAT FORTRESSES.

son had taken over several other tribes. Sometimes the Incas conquered the tribes, but other times they persuaded the tribes to join them by promising their people better lives. The Incas learned new skills in weaving, metal craft, masonry, and ceramics from several of these tribes.

By Columbus's time, the empire had spread in every direction. Called Tahuantinsuyu (Four Regions of the World), it had the high Andes Mountains, a dry coastal desert, vast, windy plains, and warmer, sheltered valleys.

➡

The vast Inca empire could not have been maintained without a good road system. Troops had to be able to reach trouble spots quickly. The Great Inca's administrators had to travel from Cuzco to faraway villages, towns, and cities to see that his orders were carried out. Roads were needed to send important messages and information from one place to another.

The Incas had no wagons, carts, or coaches. Although the wheel had been developed in Europe, the Incas hadn't got word of it yet. Llamas were plentiful in the Andes, but they were not strong enough to carry people, and the first horses still hadn't been brought to the Americas from Spain. The Great Inca and other members of royalty were carried in litters on indigenestas' shoulders. Everyone else traveled by foot.

The Andes are the second highest mountain range in the world. Steep cliffs rise sharply from low plains in

THE INCA ROAD SYSTEM WAS A MODEL
OF ENGINEERING AND EFFICIENCY.
THE ART SHOWS WHAT IS LEFT
OF SOME COMMON ROADS.

some places. Rivers have cut deep chasms between snowcapped peaks. Heavy rain, hailstorms, earthquakes, and snowslides have always been frequent. Yet Inca armies marched along what has been called one of the best road systems anywhere. Inca roads were superior to those of the ancient Romans and better than most European roads of the Incas' time.

Inca engineers tunneled through rocks, built causeways over marshes, and bridged canyons and chasms with rope as thick as a person's body. Broad steps were cut into steep hillsides so people and llamas might move more easily from one level to another.

The main mountain road stretched along the central Andes plateau for over three thousand miles from Ecuador to Argentina. That's the same as the distance between the Atlantic and Pacific coasts of the United States. The main coast road ran from Peru into Chile for two thousand miles, the same distance as the stretch between Maine and Key West, Florida. The coast road was 24 feet (about 39 km) wide and paved with flat stones to keep it from washing away or becoming muddy. Long stretches were lined with trees to shade marching warriors. Canals were dug alongside the road so the people would have fresh water to drink. *Tampus,* groups of stone buildings filled with food, clothing, and military supplies, were built a day's march from each other. Some tampus were so large that, it has been estimated,

ALONG WITH ROADS, BRIDGES WERE BUILT
TO WITHSTAND A LOT OF FOOT TRAFFIC.

as many as twenty-five thousand soldiers could eat and rest in them at the same time. Main roads were kept clear for official business. Guards were posted along the way to make sure no one traveled without permission.

Couriers called *chasquis* ran along Inca roads with messages they had memorized. The air of the Andes is too thin for people to run long distances without rest, so chasquis were trained to run short distances at top speed. Special relief stations were located within a mile or so of each other. As a chasqui drew near, he shouted or blew on a conch shell to alert the runner waiting in the station. The relief hurried out and ran at the first runner's side. The first runner repeated the message, then slowed down and allowed his relief to run ahead. The system worked so well that messages could be sent from Quito to Cuzco, a distance of 1,250 miles (2,012 km) in five days, or 250 miles (402.3 km) a day.

A folktale tells of a messenger who was often late because he stopped to help animals and people in trouble. He asked *Inti,* the Sun God, for guidance and was given a pair of magic sandals. The sandals carried him "through cities and over mountains as if on a great gust of wind," and he was never late again.

THE PEOPLE OF THE PAST

Most people ruled by the Great Inca were farmers. In some places, they cut terraces resembling steps on steep hillsides to create flat spaces on which to plant. Stones between the "steps" kept dirt from washing down when it rained. Farmers fed themselves and their families with whatever they could grow in their region. Cacao, used to make chocolate, flourished at the edge of the jungle where it was warm and damp. Beans, peanuts, and pumpkins grew in high Andes valleys. Maize and *quinoa* (an herb) also grew at high elevations. Fruits and vegetables grew in the lower valleys where the days were warm and the nights cool. Andean farmers experimented with potatoes and learned to cultivate many different kinds under various growing conditions. Potatoes were unknown in other parts of the world until the Spaniards arrived and found the Incas growing them.

Inca farmers had no machinery or animals to help

MOST INCAS WERE FARMERS.
SINCE THE PEOPLE LIVED IN
ONE OF THE MOST MOUNTAINOUS
REGIONS OF THE WORLD,
FARMING WAS DONE ON TERRACES
SUCH AS THESE PICTURED HERE.

INCAS HARVESTING
AND TRANSPORTING POTATOES.
THIS ILLUSTRATION IS FROM AN
ANCIENT PERUVIAN CODEX, A
BOOK DESCRIBING THE CUSTOMS,
RITUALS, AND LIFE OF A PEOPLE.

them. Llamas could carry small loads, but they were too delicate for harder jobs such as plowing. Farmers used a simple digging stick, a pole with a sharp point, to turn over soil before planting. Their wives often followed, breaking up sod clods with a rock attached to a shorter pole. *Guano*—the white, hardened droppings of seabirds that nested on the coast of Peru—was used for fertilizer in some places. It was once considered so valuable that anyone who killed the birds or disturbed their nesting places could be put to death.

→

A farmer's home was usually a one-room adobe hut, whether he lived in the warm coastal desert region or in the mountains. The hut had no chairs, tables, or beds. The family sat, ate, and slept on straw mats on the dirt floor. Highland nights were cold, but the hut had no stove or fireplace. The farmer's wife cooked in a shed apart from the house. The stove was made of clay and had three openings, so three neighbors could cook a one-pot meal at the same time. Dried llama dung and grass were used for fuel. Most people ate two meals a day. Breakfast was cereal or soup. Dinner was also soup, made of potatoes, corn, or quinoa, onions, squash, and any other grain or vegetable available. Meat was rarely eaten. If a llama or guinea pig was eaten for a special occasion, the leftover meat was dried in the sun to preserve it for another time. Dried meat was called *charqui* and is still eaten in Peru. The English work "jerky" comes from that Quechua word.

Inca farmers devised a way of freeze-drying potatoes so they could be stored for as long as five or six years without spoiling. They set the potatoes out in the freezing night air and defrosted them the next day in the warm noonday sun. The farmer's wife pressed out the moisture with her feet. This process was repeated until the potatoes dried into a thick white chunk that looked like plastic foam. When the family needed potatoes, the chunk was soaked in water and cooked. Called *chuño*, freeze-dried potatoes are eaten to this day in Peru.

➡

One of the tribes the Incas defeated was called the *Chimus*. They had built fine towns and irrigated fields near rivers on the eastern edge of the coastal desert before the Incas defeated them. Most Chimus lived on the coastal desert and made their living by fishing in the Pacific Ocean. A cool ocean current, called the Humboldt Current, brought many fish to their waters. Chimu fishermen caught several different kinds of fish, from giant rays and sharks to tiny anchovies. The Chimus dried the anchovies and ground them into fishmeal to fertilize their fields. Mussels, crabs, and clams were also abundant along the shore.

Clay pots in museums show pictures of fishermen lowering fishhooks into the sea at the end of strings.

They didn't use rods as we do today. Their boats were made of tortora reeds tied into bundles and fastened together. Some reed boats were no larger than bathtubs. They functioned all right in good weather but became waterlogged when it rained and were easily lost or sunk in sudden ocean storms. Reed boats were more practical for fishing on Lake Titicaca and are still used there.

The Chimus also made rafts of balsa wood that had been stripped of its branches and bark. Some rafts had square sails which made them steadier and more reliable in the water. Some large rafts were built with little huts so the fishermen could have shade from the hot sun. Similar rafts were used for trading up and down the coast. Thor Heyerdahl, the explorer-archaeologist of *Kon-Tiki* fame, proved that a balsa raft could be navigated from Lima, Peru, across the Pacific as far as the Tuamotu Islands, a distance of about 4,000 miles (6,437 km).

Chimu houses were built of sun-dried brick with thatched roofs. Poorer people built huts by stretching reed mats around wooden frames or by standing three old reed boats on end and tying them together on top to make a kind of tent.

The Chimus worshiped *Pachacamac,* God of the Sea, because he provided them with fish. They couldn't understand why the Incas worshiped the Sun God. The noonday sun on the coastal desert was so hot the Chi-

THE CHIMUS, A TRIBE DEFEATED
BY THE INCAS, SAILED ON BOATS
AND RAFTS MADE OF BALSA WOOD.

mus took any shade from it that they could find. Chimus wore very little clothing because of the heat. Sometimes young people wore nothing at all.

→

Indigenestas in cool mountain climates wore clothes woven of llama, alpaca, or sheep's wool. Most people had two sets of clothing, one for everyday wear, and one for festivals. Men wore loincloths under sleeveless shirts that hung down to their knees. Their woolen capes served as blankets at night.

Noblemen's shirts were woven of fine vicuña wool by the best weavers in the empire. The Great Inca's cloak was made of bright-colored bird feathers. Archaeologists have found a gold crown that they think may have been worn by Huayna Capac, the last reigning Inca. The Inca Pachacuti has been pictured wearing a headband called an *allantu*. It had a scarlet fringe, and feathers were fastened to the front of it by a gold brooch. Smaller feathers hung almost down to Pachacuti's eyebrows. Noblemen and the Great Inca wore large gold earrings, called earplugs, which stretched out their earlobes and gave them the nickname "Long Ears." A Spanish writer wrote that the Great Inca wore his clothes only once and then burned them as an offering to his father, the Sun God.

The Sun God was second only to *Viracocha,* the Incas' God of Creation. The Great Inca always consulted his priests before making important decisions, such

VARIOUS HEADDRESSES
OF THE ANCIENT PERUVIANS

NOBLEMEN AND THE
GREAT INCA WORE MANY
ORNAMENTS, INCLUDING
OCCASIONALLY NOSE
ORNAMENTS AND EARRINGS
SUCH AS THESE. NOTICE
THE WARRIOR CARRYING
A VICTIM'S HEAD.

as which day would be best for waging war, sowing seed, or taking a wife. The priests maintained temples, conducted ceremonies, and made offerings to gods. In times of great trouble such as famine or epidemic, a child or young person might be sacrificed instead of the usual llama or guinea pig.

The moon and other wonders of nature were also huaca (sacred). These included certain mountain peaks, rocks, springs, and plants. A man trudging through a dangerous mountain pass would add a small stone to a pile built up by other travelers, so that the god of the mountain would help him reach home safely.

The Incas' special medicine men, the Calloways, traveled through the Andes with bags of charms to help people solve problems and with herbs to heal the sick. Archaeologists have dug up silver crowns for capping teeth and skulls that show that brain surgery was performed at the time.

➡

Scientists think astronomers observed the sun, moon, and stars from four stone towers east and west of Cuzco to work out the Inca calendar. It was divided into twelve months, with each month thirty days long. Instead of having seven days, the Inca week had ten days, so each month had three weeks instead of four.

Seasons south of the Equator are reversed, so January on the Inca calendar corresponded to June in North

THIS CHIMU FEATHERED
NECK PIECE IS AN
EXAMPLE OF THE
INCAN INFLUENCE
AND STYLE. IT SHOWS
VIRACOCHA, THE INCA
GOD OF CREATION.

A MURAL BY ALTON TOBEY
DEPICTS BRAIN SURGERY
PERFORMED BY THE INCAS.

AN INCA ZODIAC OF GOLD

THIS MAGNIFICENT SIGHT
IS THE SOLAR CLOCK
AT MACHU PICCHU.

America. *Inti Raymi*, Festival of the Sun, was held in June and lasted nine days. During Inti Raymi, the Incas believed the Sun God was the host, and the nobility, the guests. Each year the Great Inca sat at the top of the Sun Temple's steps and watched the ceremony. Musicians blew trumpets, whistles, and flutes made of bone, reed, shell, and metal. Men and women joined hands and moved across the plaza to the rhythm of a huge drum made of llama hide stretched tightly across a wooden frame. At daybreak on the fourth day, priests stretched out their arms, pursed their lips, and made kissing noises to the Sun God. Pictures illustrating Spanish records show priests offering the Sun God *chicha*, beer made of fermented corn or quinoa. On the Inca calendar, January was called the Month of Small Ripening; February, the Month of Great Ripening; March, the Month of Flowers and Earth Ripening; and May, the Month of Harvest.

→

During *Kapac Raymi*, Magnificent Festival, in December, the sons of the nobility were initiated into the Great Inca's service.

As the empire expanded, the government in Cuzco had to train boys to become army generals and priests. Thousands of administrators were needed to see that the Great Inca's orders were carried out. Noblemen's sons started this training at about the age of twelve. Sinchi Roca, either the first or second Inca (depending on

TOP: THE INTERIOR OF A
TEMPLE OF THE SUN AS IT MIGHT
HAVE LOOKED. THE SUN GOD
WAS NEXT IN IMPORTANCE
AFTER THE GOD OF CREATION.
BOTTOM: INTI RAYMI, THE INCA
SUN FESTIVAL, HELD IN JUNE,
IS STILL A CAUSE FOR
CELEBRATION TODAY.

whether the first one was actually real or a legendary figure), founded a university to educate sons of nobles. Because the Incas had no written language we know of, teachers taught the empire's history from memory. Schoolchildren in Peru still memorize the names of all the Great Incas and recite them in the games they play.

The sons of noblemen learned how to use and understand the *quipu,* the Incas' counting system. A counter, something like the Chinese abacus, was used to add and subtract. Totals were recorded on the quipu, which consisted of a main cord about a yard long, with shorter, knotted strings of various colors hanging from it. Math-

THE INCA DICTATING IN HIS SCHOOL.
NOBLEMEN'S SONS WERE TRAINED
BOTH TO BECOME OFFICERS IN THE
ARMY AND ADMINISTRATORS TO CARRY
OUT THE GREAT INCA'S ORDERS.

THE QUIPU,
THE DEVICE USED BY
THE INCAS TO COUNT

ematicians think the knots probably represented numbers, and the spaces between the knots stood for zero. Hundreds of quipus enabled the government to keep track of important matters such as how much food had to be harvested and ready for its storehouses, how many soldiers were needed to defend and expand the empire, or how many men should be recruited to work in mines.

➡

Each year as many as six hundred girls between the ages of eight and twelve were selected to become Sun Maidens, or Chosen Women. A Spanish author wrote that the girls were chosen for their beauty, grace, and intelligence, and to be picked was considered an honor. The girls went to live in a gray, forbidding building surrounded by a high wall and guarded by soldiers. Any boy or man caught nearby was severely punished.

Some of the girls later married noblemen or warriors. Others lived in the temple, where they wove the priests' clothing, prepared their food, and helped with religious ceremonies. Some girls went to live in the Great Inca's palace and catered to his needs. Others were sacrificed to the gods in times of trouble.

Most children had no formal education, but were taught only by their parents. At two or three years of age, boys learned to carry water and feed the animals. By nine, they prepared the earth, planted, weeded, watered, fertilized, harvested, and traded some of their

A CEREMONIAL VASE OF
A WARRIOR WITH A CLUB

produce at market. Girls learned to spin, weave, cook, clean, and care for younger brothers and sisters.

➡

Money was unknown in the days of the empire. Gold, called "Sweat of the Sun," and silver, called "Tears of the Moon," were *huaca* and prized only for their beauty. *Mita,* service, was the Inca way of collecting taxes. Every able-bodied person was obliged to give some sort of service to the state. Farmers donated part of their harvest and craftsmen some of their wares. Men worked on roads or in mines. Some built bridges, fortifications, and public buildings. Most served in the army at some time in their lives.

END OF THE EMPIRE

In 1532, news spread throughout the empire that some bearded white men had landed on the northern coast of Peru. The Quechuas had heard about bearded white men who had ruled the natives near Lake Titicaca long before the Incas did. Storytellers said the white men could do such wonderful things that the natives thought they were gods. Then the Incas came and claimed that they themselves were the only gods. To prove it, the Incas killed some of the white men. Others escaped, and for centuries the Quechuas expected them to return. No one knew where the earlier white men came from. The Quechuas thought those who had just landed were the same ones.

Their leader was a Spaniard named Francisco Pizarro. He had heard about the gold, silver, and precious stones with which the Incas decorated their buildings.

Pizarro and his men, taking horses and the cannon, left their ship and started inland.

By this time millions of natives had died of diseases which had been brought to their shores by Spanish ships that had landed earlier. Smallpox was probably the principal killer. The natives had never been exposed to scarlet fever, measles, or bubonic plague either, and they had no natural immunity or medicines to cure them. In 1525 Huayna Capac, the Great Inca himself, fell ill and died.

One of his sons, Atahualpa, ruled the northern portion of the empire from Quito at the time. A second son, Huascar, ruled the south from Cuzco. Both brothers claimed to be the rightful ruler of the entire empire, and they fought a war called the "War of Two Brothers." The war lasted for five years. Atahualpa finally won and was on his way to Cuzco to claim the whole kingdom when he and his soldiers met Pizarro and his armored soldiers and horses in the mountains. Had Pizarro tried to invade the Inca empire five years before, he would have been confronted with a strong, united people instead of a country that had just fought a civil war. The Incas might have won.

Pizarro tricked Atahualpa into thinking the Spaniards meant no harm, and took him hostage. They kept him imprisoned for eight months. He would be set free

THE ARRIVAL OF THE WHITE MEN
SPELLED THE EVENTUAL DEMISE OF THE
INCA EMPIRE. THIS PAINTING DEPICTS A
MEETING BETWEEN THE SPANISH LEADER
PIZARRO AND ATAHUALPA, THE INCA LEADER
WHOM THE SPANISH LATER KILLED.

in return for a roomful of gold and two roomfuls of silver, Pizarro said. A book later written by a Spaniard shows a sketch of an Inca asking a Spanish soldier if Spaniards ate gold, since they seemed to want it so much. More than twenty-four tons of treasure were collected and given to the conquistadores for Atahualpa's freedom. The conquistadores took the money and killed Atahualpa anyway.

The Inca empire collapsed. Pizarro named himself governor and crowned another of Atahualpa's brothers Great Inca because the brother seemed to be an easygoing man who would act as a puppet in carrying out Pizarro's orders. Spanish people came and took over Inca lands, mines, temples, fortresses, storehouses, and whatever else they could get their hands on. Indigenestas were forced to work in Spanish homes and fields, as well as carry heavy loads long distances over the mountains. Worst of all was *mita de minas,* service in the mines. Everyone went into mourning when men from a certain village were drafted to work at Potosi, a silver mine in Bolivia. Miners worked deep in the earth in unbearable heat. Each man had to dig twenty-five hundred-pound sacks of ore a day or he would be whipped. Frequent cave-ins buried alive thousands.

Several rebellions took place. A statue in Cochabamba, Bolivia, honors those women who fought with sticks and stones against the Spaniards.

IN ONLY A FEW SHORT YEARS, THE
SPANISH DESTROYED WHAT HAD TAKEN
THE INCAS MANY YEARS TO BUILD.
THIS IS AN EXAMPLE OF SPANISH
BUILDINGS BUILT ATOP INCA WALLS.

Tupac Amaru, the last puppet emperor, led a failed rebellion in 1572. The Spanish governor tore out the Inca's tongue, and made him watch while four horses driven in different directions pulled the limbs of his wife and sons apart. Then Tupac Amaru was killed, too.

Although Sacsahuamán, the fort outside Cuzco, had taken about sixty years to build, the Spaniards disassembled most of it in only a few years. They also tore down buildings around Cuzco's square and used stones from Sacsahuamán to build Spanish-style buildings over the Inca foundations. Earthquakes have toppled some of the Spanish structures over the years. But the foundations of Inca buildings and part of Sacsahuamán's wall still stand strong and intact.

THE PEOPLE TODAY

Descendants of people who lived under the richest, most powerful empire in the New World are now among the poorest people on earth. Many live in tiny villages high in the Andes, where the climate is so harsh it is impossible to make a decent living. The houses are made of mud with thatched roofs and many have no windows or just small square holes with no glass. There are no fireplaces or chimneys in most of the houses. Many have no furniture or only a few homemade pieces. Vast areas are without electricity or running water. There are few schools and little or no transportation.

Miners work underground where it is so hot they have to constantly spray themselves with water. A tunnel might cave in at any time, or dynamite could explode accidentally and kill everyone in the area. Indigenestas living along the Amazon River are forced to leave their homes because cattle and lumbermen are taking over the land.

Thousands of Andean people move to towns or cities hoping to make a better life for themselves and their children. With no money and no place to live, they set up little shacks in crowded slums and try to find work. Jobs for uneducated people are scarce, and men still work like pack animals, their backs bent over with heavy loads strapped to them. Disease spreads quickly in crowded, unsanitary conditions. Cholera broke out in 1991 and many people died.

According to law, everyone is supposed to go to school through the third grade. Many children don't go at all. Some drop out after one or two grades because they are needed to work at home or their families need any money they might be able to earn. City boys shine shoes, run errands, and change tires. City girls work in factories, clean people's houses, or try to sell wares to tourists.

➡

In some parts of the Andes, women's clothes have changed little over the past four hundred years. Many women still make their own clothing, including the fabric. One rarely sees a woman or girl walking along a mountain road or tending a flock without a whirling spindle in her hand. She's spinning wool with which to make fabric. One hand twists the spindle while the other

[49]

MUCH HAS NOT CHANGED FOR THE
PEOPLE OF THE ANDES. THIS WOMAN IN
TRADITIONAL INDIAN CLOTHING WEAVES,
JUST AS HER ANCESTORS DID DURING
THE HEIGHT OF THE INCA EMPIRE.

feeds the wool and thins it out. The fabric is then woven on old-fashioned looms strapped around the weavers' waists, just as was done in the days of the empire. Many families can't afford a sewing machine, so clothes are often sewn by hand.

Andean men and boys wear ponchos similar to those worn in the past, but their trousers and shirts are more like those of Americans. Men in Bolivia's highlands wear plain, dark woolen jackets and matching knee-length pants. They often go barefoot.

→

Tiny woven pouches hold coca leaves from bushes that grow on the eastern slopes of the Andes. In the time of the empire, coca leaves were considered huaca and only the Great Inca, nobles, and priests were allowed to chew them. Some people think the Spaniards encouraged indigenestas to chew the leaves because they contain cocaine which enables people to work longer hours without food or rest. Nowadays, many Andeans chew the leaves to keep from feeling hungry on their meager diet. It also prevents them from feeling exhausted while working so hard in thin mountain air.

Inca and Spanish rulers shifted indigenestas from place to place to provide workers where needed and prevent revolts. The rulers insisted that everyone from a certain area wear the same kind of hat so they could be identified. Many people from the same area still wear them. Aymara women wear brown or black English-style derbies. Quechua women wear tall black or white "stovepipe" styles, such as Abraham Lincoln's famous hat. The ribbons around the crown show whether the woman is single, married, or a widow. White "stovepipes" look like paper or straw. They are really made of tightly crocheted thread that is then starched, blocked, and painted white. In Sucre, Bolivia, some men wear felt hats shaped like the conquistadores' metal helmets. Men of Taquile Island on Lake Titicaca walk around knitting their own floppy woolen hats. In the village of Pisac, Peru, women wear colorful round hats.

Saturday or Sunday is market day in many places, and the whole family usually participates. The marketplace bustles with activity as people arrive by truck, bus, bicycle, mule, ox cart, or on foot. Llamas carry loads of up to a hundred pounds. Mules carry more. Children greet friends as they help unload things their families have brought to sell or trade. A teenage boy lines up sandals he has made from old tires. His sister spreads out baskets and mats she has woven from leaves. Her mother spreads out her hand-woven blankets.

Children sell clay beads they have painted and strung together to make necklaces. A husband and wife set out pots molded of clay dug from a riverbank near their home. Some native artisans display paper-thin ceramics

A VILLAGE MARKET IS A BUSY PLACE,
FILLED WITH ALL KINDS OF NATIVE CRAFTS.

they have painted with strands of their own hair instead of paintbrushes.

If a person wishes to buy tomatoes at the market-place in La Paz, Bolivia, she goes to the section where only tomatoes are sold. If she needs toothpaste, she goes to the toothpaste area. One vendor may have hundreds of chili peppers to sell. Another may have four frying pans. A private organization based in the United States gives small loans to vendors in the Rodriguez Market in La Paz so they can buy better merchandise and earn more money. The lenders use a kind of sharing mita system, which means four people must apply for one vendor's loan. Each vendor vouches for the others and promises to pay if the other borrowers don't. Vendors pay back the loans little by little. A fifty-dollar loan usually increases a vendor's income from 50 to 100 percent, and more than 99 percent of the borrowers have paid back their loans.

➜

The Spaniards declared public Inca religious festivals unlawful and forced natives to become Catholic. The Incas managed to keep some of their old customs by combining a number of religious practices. During Inti Raymi, villagers may have a Catholic priest sprinkle their rundown cars or trucks with holy water to keep the engines running. A boy in a white robe, wearing a brightly striped cloak and "golden" crown like those of a Great

Inca, may follow the Virgin Mary's statue as it is carried through the street on a Catholic holiday.

Yma, a girl playing jacks and selling sweaters outside a Cuzco hotel, watches a play performed every year at Inti Raymi. The play is about an Inca hero who is killed by bearded white men. At the end of the play, the Inca rises from the dead, restores the empire's glory, and makes better lives for his people. This will never come to pass, of course, and although the governments of countries once ruled by Incas frequently change, none has improved indigenestas' lives very much.

GLOSSARY

Allantu (ah lan′ tu)   Great Inca's headband

Aymaras (I mah′ ras)   people who speak Aymara language

Campesinos (cam pe see′ nos)   small farmers

Charqui (char′ key)   dried meat

Chasquis (chas′ keys)   runners

Chicha (chee′ chah)   alcoholic beverage made from fermented quinoa or corn

Chimus (Chee′ moos)   a tribe conquered by the Incas

Chuño (choo′ nyu)   freeze-dried potatoes

Conquistadores (con kee′ sta dor ees)   Spanish conquerors

Guano (gwa' no)   dried excrement of seabirds and bats found mixed with feathers and bones; used as a fertilizer

Huaca (wah' kah)   sacred, when used as an adjective; sacred person or thing, as a noun

Indigenestas (in di jen ees' tas)   commoners or people not of noble birth

Inti (In' tee)   Sun God

Inti Raymi (In' tee Ray' mee)   Sun Festival

Kapac Raymi (Ka' pak Ray' mee)   Magnificent Festival

Mita (mee' ta)   service

Mita de minas (mee'ta de mee' nas)   service in the mines

Pachacamac (Pa cha ka' mak)   God of the Sea

Quechuas (Kesh waz')   people who speak the language of Queshua

Quinoa (keen' wah)   herb whose seeds provide staple food; it is eaten boiled like rice and used in soup or porridge; it is fermented to make chicha

Quipu (kee' puh)   Inca account-keeping system

Runas (Roo' nas)   natives

Tampus (tam' poos)   storehouses

Viracocha (vee' ra ko' cha)   God of Creation

FOR FURTHER READING

Bleeker, Sonia. *The Inca Indians of the Andes*. New York: Morrow Jr. Books, 1960.

Burland, C. A. *Finding Out About the Incas*. New York: Lothrop, Lee and Shepherd, 1962.

McIntyre, Loren. *The Incredible Incas and Their Timeless Land*. Washington, D.C.: National Geographic Society, 1975.

Marrin, Albert. *Inca and Spaniard, Pizarro and the Conquest of Peru*. New York: Atheneum, 1989.

Von Hagen, Victor W. *The Incas, People of the Sun*. Cleveland and New York: World, 1961.

INDEX

[60]